CONTEMPORARY LIVES

LADY GAGA

POP SINGER & SONGWRITER

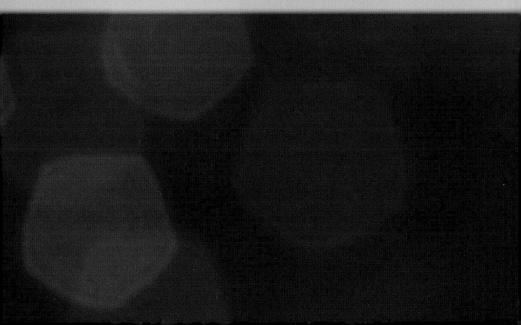

ABDO
Publishing Company

LADY GAGA

POP SINGER & SONGWRITER

by Katie Marsico

CREDITS

Published by ABDO Publishing Company, PO Box 398166, Minneapolis, MN 55439. Copyright © 2012 by Abdo Consulting Group, Inc. International copyrights reserved in all countries. No part of this book may be reproduced in any form without written permission from the publisher. The Essential Library™ is a trademark and logo of ABDO Publishing Company.

Printed in the United States of America,
North Mankato, Minnesota
112011
012012

Editor: Lisa Owings
Copy Editor: Mari Kesselring
Design and production: Emily Love

Library of Congress Cataloging-in-Publication Data
Marsico, Katie, 1980-
  Lady Gaga : pop singer & songwriter / by Katie Marsico.
    p. cm. -- (Contemporary lives)
  Includes bibliographical references.
  ISBN 978-1-61783-324-3
  1. Lady Gaga--Juvenile literature. 2. Singers--United States--
Biography--Juvenile literature. I. Title.
  ML3930.L13M37 2012
  782.42164092--dc23
  [B]
                                                    2011040469

TABLE OF CONTENTS

In 2009, Lady Gaga took her performance art around the world with her Fame Ball Tour.

CHAPTER 1

Debut Tour or Traveling Party?

||||||||||||||||||||||||||||||||||||||||

From March to September 2009, audiences across the world were dazzled by a concert tour unlike anything they had ever seen onstage. The 69 performances Lady Gaga gave in North America, Europe, Oceania, and Asia were bold, dazzling, and— much like the pop artist herself—highly unique. The Fame Ball Tour was Lady

Gaga's debut concert tour. The tour was intended to help promote her first studio album, *The Fame*. From the beginning, however, Lady Gaga made it clear she wanted audiences to do more than simply listen to a few up-and-coming pop songs at her concerts. As she explained during an interview with MTV News,

> *It's not really a tour. It's more of a traveling party. I want it to be an entire experience from [the] minute you walk in [the] front door to [the] minute I begin to sing. And, when it's all over, everyone's going to press rewind and relive it again.[1]*

As audiences and critics discovered, Lady Gaga would not disappoint them.

Her costumes were elaborate and bizarre, ranging from a dress made of plastic bubbles to a khaki leotard that sparkled with crystals.

TOURING AND TIME TRAVELING |||||||||||||||||||||||||||||||||||||||||||||

While promoting her Fame Ball Tour, Lady Gaga promised fans, "It's going to be as if you're walking into New York circa 1974: There's an art installation in the lobby, a DJ spinning your favorite records in the main room, and then the most haunting performance that you've ever seen on the stage."[2]

Dazzling pyrotechnics lit up the stage during Lady Gaga's performances.

During the performance, she played the piano wearing stiletto heels as she sat next to glowing mannequins. Giant video screens, pyrotechnics, and disco lights were just a sampling of the special effects adding to the onstage extravaganza that wowed fans.

As for Lady Gaga's music and lyrics, they are as intriguing as the shimmering visual spectacle that accompanied them. She sang about fame, a topic musical artists have focused on for hundreds of years. Yet Lady Gaga's lyrics also reference everything from far-off planets to disco beats to paparazzi photographers.

Lady Gaga's electropop rhythms are clearly influenced by the stylings of chart toppers, including Michael Jackson, Madonna, and Britney Spears. What did critics say about Lady Gaga's unusual but entrancing blend of, what one reviewer described as, "music, fashion, art, and technology"?[3] Even so-so reviews of the Fame Ball Tour praised Lady Gaga for her performance. "Her onstage banter was at times a bit silly," noted a critic from *Entertainment Weekly*. The critic went on:

> But her voice was strong and refreshingly free of overbearing . . . vocals. For all her cocky bluster,

BRASH, BRIGHT, AND SLIGHTLY STRANGE

Journalist Hattie Collins of London, England's, *Sunday Times* noted *The Fame* is "a fantastic mix of [David] Bowie-esque ballads, dramatic, Queen-inspired . . . numbers and synth-based dance tracks that poke fun at celebrity-chasing rich kids."[4] She also praised the debut album as being "entertaining, incredibly witty, and, above all, captivating."[5] As for the performer herself, Collins described Lady Gaga as a "perplexing, somewhat camp combination of brash, bright, and slightly strange."[6]

Lady Gaga's creative costumes from the Fame Ball Tour proved how endlessly innovative she could be.

perhaps *the most undeniable aspect of Gaga's talent is this: The girl can, and does, sing.*[7]

Meanwhile, a different reviewer from *Billboard* remarked, "[From] her chart success, Lady Gaga has proven herself to be an of-the-moment pop sensation. Dig deeper, and it's clear she's versatile

COMFORTABLE BEING SELF-CONFIDENT

Lady Gaga doesn't have a problem showing the world she believes in herself as a pop star and a performance artist. During a 2011 interview with *Vogue*, she told a reporter:

"Speaking purely from a musical standpoint, I think I am a great performer. I am a talented entertainer. I consider myself to have one of the greatest voices in the industry. I consider myself to be one of the greatest songwriters. I wouldn't say that I am one of the greatest dancers, but I am really quite good at what I do. I think it's OK to be confident in yourself."[9]

and talented enough to have staying power."[8] Time—and Lady Gaga's musical creativity and fearless stage presence—would soon prove how truly accurate that observation was.

CHART TOPPER AND INDUSTRY CHANGER

The pop sensation known as Lady Gaga spent years working in music clubs and experiencing her share of professional growth and heartbreak before she found success. Finally, the chairman of a California-based record label took a chance and signed her. Although Lady Gaga initially built her career as a songwriter for other musicians, *The Fame* provided her with an opportunity to demonstrate her remarkable skills as a performance artist. It was this album that helped her rise to the top of the charts in six countries and win acclaim with fans across the globe.

Over the next few years, Lady Gaga debuted two additional albums and continued to make a name for herself as a leading stage and recording artist. In February 2011, she set music-industry records with the single "Born This Way." Within five days of its release, the track sold more than 1 million copies. In addition, Lady Gaga has been nominated for numerous awards and has enjoyed multiple wins, including winning five Grammy Awards.

A BIG-NAME RECORD BREAKER |||||||||||||||||||||||||||||||

Lady Gaga is the first recording artist to enjoy four Number 1 hits with a debut album. The songs "Just Dance," "Poker Face," "LoveGame," and "Paparazzi" are all featured on *The Fame*. The songs became chart toppers in 2008 and 2009. Lady Gaga fans have bought more than 15 million copies of *The Fame* since its release.

Lady Gaga performed at the American Music Awards
on November 22, 2009.

Just as important, Lady Gaga has rocked the
world music scene with her unusual and often
shocking take on performance artistry and the
meaning of fame. Audiences are drawn to her
startling artistic flair and bold self-expression.
Lady Gaga has also become recognized as a
champion of the gay and lesbian community. She
is both a performer and a person who is unafraid
to be different. Her celebrity and influence have
encouraged others to accept and embrace people's

Shortly after kicking off her Fame Ball Tour, Lady Gaga spoke to reporters about why her songs represented more than just music. She said:

> "This is all part of a movement. My artistry is much deeper than fashion or anything like that: I love pop music, and I want to bring it back. People are truly hungry for this. They generally miss the 90s and the superfans flooding Times Square, crying and wailing and doing anything to see the fingernail of a star. I want that back."[10]

Lady Gaga went on to further express confidence in her performance art and the fact that she was helping return pop music to its former glory. She explained:

> "[Pop music] is back. I promise you. It's happening right now. My work is honest and strong, and I couldn't be [happier] to see it reach so many people."[11]

differences. Though she appears to have a long and fulfilling career ahead of her, Lady Gaga has already achieved enormous success. She has also demonstrated her ability to send a meaningful message to the public—both on- and offstage.

||||||||||||

Stefani was born and raised in New York City and can often be spotted there by her fans.

CHAPTER 2

Early Steps toward Stardom

||||||||||||||||||||||||||||||||||||||||||||||||||||

tefani Joanne Angelina
Germanotta was born in
New York City on March
28, 1986, to Italian-American parents
Joseph and Cynthia Germanotta. The
Germanottas welcomed a second
daughter, Natali, a little less than
six years later. Stefani's mother and
father worked hard to make sure the

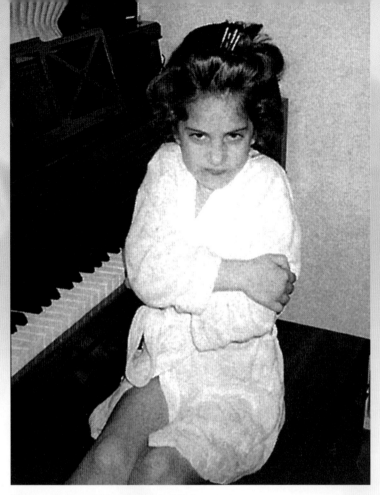

Stefani showed talent as a musician and entertainer from a young age.

family could live in a duplex in an upper-class neighborhood on Manhattan's Upper West Side.

Stefani's parents also paid for private lessons so the future Lady Gaga could further develop what was already an obvious musical talent. Stefani was only four years old when she taught herself how to play the piano by ear. Once she began lessons, she practiced with fierce determination, routinely sitting at the piano bench for much longer than her parents and teachers told her she had to practice.

Yet Stefani didn't look at these efforts as a chore. She adored music, and it made up a huge part of her life from an incredibly young age. Using her plastic cassette player as backup music, she belted out hits by pop artists Michael Jackson and Cyndi Lauper. When Stefani wasn't working on her vocals, she could often be found dancing with her father to songs by British rockers such as the Rolling Stones or the Beatles. Even fancy New York restaurants provided opportunities for the little girl to perform. Stefani wasn't shy about transforming breadsticks into batons and dancing around the dinner tables.

A FLAIR FOR DRAMA

Stefani was inspired to act from the time she was a child. Taking acting classes at age 11 helped her learn how to use her imagination to develop her dramatic abilities. "I remember the first time that I drank out of an imaginary coffee cup," she recollected as an adult. "That's the very first thing they teach you. I can feel the rain, too, when it's not raining."[1]

Stefani was only 13 years old when she composed her first piano ballad. Within a year, she was participating in open-mic nights at local music clubs. As she would prove on much bigger stages years later, Stefani's talent wasn't the only part of her identity that made her stand out. She had a distinctive personality and style that easily separated her from the rest of the crowd.

"I was always an entertainer. . . . I was a ham as a little girl, and I'm a ham today."[2]

—LADY GAGA

STANDING OUT IN SCHOOL

While Stefani's family supported her early performance efforts, not everyone was a huge fan of the young musician. In fact, she later insisted she had few friends during her time at the Convent of the Sacred Heart School on Manhattan's Upper East Side. Stefani's parents worked hard to pay for her tuition there, and, in turn, she was a dedicated

Stefani took her early stage efforts quite seriously. In fact, she often refused to respond to her real name backstage during school performances. Instead, she insisted cast mates call her by the name of whatever character she happened to be playing. The teen actress also tended to speak to other performers offstage in the same voice and manner she used onstage.

student. Nevertheless, day-to-day life at the upper-class private school sometimes proved a challenge for the teenager.

"I always gravitated to different things," she recalled during an interview. "I was eccentric. I went to a school full of spoiled kids. [They made fun of] the way I dressed and talked."[3] One of her classmates later claimed some of this bullying resulted from jealousy over her being cast as the lead in school musicals.

"[Older girls stuck in the chorus] always talked behind her back," the friend recalled. "[They said things] like, 'Gross, she's the Germ! She's dirty!'"[4] Yet this didn't stop Stefani from pushing ahead with her dream to perform. Having taken acting lessons from age 11, she didn't find it difficult to win starring roles in school plays. Stefani even created a demo CD that was filled with recordings of her own love songs. The Germanottas handed out copies of the CD as favors at a sweet 16 birthday party they threw her.

> "Everyone [who] was playing her demo [was] like, "Whoa, she's going to be a star." She was by far the most talented person in high school, but she'd do so many random acts of kindness, like saying [to other performers], 'Your singing has gotten so much better. You're working hard and I've noticed.' She wasn't a diva at all."[5]
>
> —A CLASSMATE RECALLING STEFANI GERMANOTTA'S DEMO CD

HARDWORKING AND WILLING TO TAKE RISKS

At school, Stefani had a reputation for not being a diva. This may have been because Stefani had to work hard for what she wanted. The Germanottas lived in an upscale Manhattan neighborhood and sent their daughters to a posh private school, but their eldest child still had to get a job. Stefani found employment as a waitress in a restaurant on the Upper West Side.

While she had a tight-knit relationship with her family, Stefani sometimes raised their eyebrows. Her teachers occasionally scolded her for wearing low-cut shirts or what they considered inappropriate clothing. During high school, Stefani started dating an older boy, bought a fake ID, and got her first tattoo. "That's part of why I needed a job after school, too," she later joked. "My dad wouldn't give me money to go out on the weekends because he knew I was going downtown and being bad."[6] For the most part, though, the girl who would one day become Lady Gaga managed to stay out of serious trouble.

After graduating from high school in 2004, Stefani enrolled in New York University's (NYU)

WORKING TO AFFORD FASHION

Fashion intrigued Stefani from an early age, which was part of the reason she started waitressing as a teenager. Years later she would recall the joy she experienced when she could finally afford to buy a Gucci purse during high school. "I was so excited because all the girls at Sacred Heart always had their fancy purses," she noted. "I always had 'whatever.' My mom and dad were not buying me a $600 purse."[7]

Though Stefani would ultimately experience her share of ups and downs with her parents—especially her father—as she journeyed toward becoming Lady Gaga, they remain extremely close. As evidence of this fact, Cynthia Germanotta has been known to accompany her eldest daughter on tour. Even after achieving celebrity status, Stefani said her relationship with her parents essentially stayed much the same as it did when she shared a duplex with them in Manhattan.

Tisch School of the Arts. The program had an excellent reputation, and the curriculum was rigorous. Stefani focused on drama, which meant she took a wide range of classes offering instruction in everything from acting and singing to dancing and art. It didn't take long, however, before she realized Tisch wasn't exactly what she was looking for.

Stefani reasoned, "Once you learn how to think about art, you can teach yourself."[8] Stefani returned home during her sophomore year of college and announced to her parents that she was dropping out of school at Tisch. Stefani also confronted her family with an announcement that was going to

Joseph and Cynthia Germanotta maintain
a close relationship with their rock star daughter.

change the rest of her life—she had decided to
become a rock star.

||||||||||

Lady Gaga performs at Madison Square Garden in Manhattan, where she grew up and began her music career.

CHAPTER 3

Chasing Her Dreams

||||||||||||||||||||||||||||||||||||||||||||||

Germanotta didn't look at her time off from school as an opportunity to kick back, relax, and decide what her future might hold. In fact, she was already quite sure what she wanted out of life, and it involved landing a record deal by the time she turned 21. Yet her father offered to pay for her rent for just one year—and with the understanding that she would return to college if her rock-and-roll

STARTING OFF SIMPLE |||||||||||||||||||||||||||||||||||||||||||||||||||||||||||||||||||||||||

Since Germanotta was resistant to the idea of living off of her parents' money after leaving college, her first apartment was by no means glamorous. Yet she decorated it as best she could, with a futon serving as her couch. Germanotta also added little touches here and there that reflected her taste in music and her desire to develop her own identity as a performer. For example, she hung a single record by musician and activist Yoko Ono from the ceiling over her bed.

ambitions failed to materialize within that period. Meanwhile, Germanotta realized her dreams were not likely to unfold without a lot of hard work— and possibly a little heartache.

"You've got to play clubs," she later explained of what it takes to become a star performer. "You've got to do amazing, you've got to fail, you've got to get standing ovations and need to be booed off the stage."[1] While Germanotta braced herself for what she already knew might be a rocky road to fame, she settled into her new New York City apartment on Manhattan's Lower East Side. In addition to changing her address, she also began making a few adjustments to her physical appearance. Perhaps the most obvious of these was her new hairstyle.

She straightened her curly blonde locks and dyed them black.

Not wanting to rely on her parents for money, Germanotta did everything from waitressing at a local café to go-go dancing at a burlesque bar. She also formed her own band. The Stefani Germanotta Band, or SGBand, included a few of her former classmates from NYU. Along with guitarist Eli Silverman, bassist Calvin Pia, and drummer Alex Beckman, Germanotta created her own ballads, which some listeners compared to the stylings of singer Fiona Apple. The group also performed classic rock songs by bands such as Led Zeppelin. The SGBand toured a variety of Manhattan clubs and bars and eventually started building a small fan following.

SINGING IN A BASEMENT STUDIO

The first music studio Germanotta spent time in was not exactly a posh hangout for celebrity recording artists. She and the SGBand initially developed their demos in the basement of a New Jersey liquor store. The modest studio belonged to a producer named Joe Vulpis, who had watched Germanotta perform and was impressed by what he heard and saw.

WAITING TO GET NOTICED

To the roughly 20 fans who applauded the SGBand as they toured Manhattan's club scene, the performer who would one day become Lady Gaga was a sensation. Not everyone felt the same way, though. The deadline Germanotta's father had set for her return to school was fast approaching in early 2006. While she had formed her own band and was busily supporting herself until she made it to the big time, she wasn't there yet.

Meanwhile, Joseph Germanotta had started to suspect his daughter had lost her mind. When he watched her perform in her jet-black hair and a skimpy leotard, he became concerned. To him, the performer he saw onstage was a disturbingly different person from the girl who had so recently been on the cusp of a promising future at NYU.

STRUGGLING TO SELF-PROMOTE

Self-promotion is hard work, as Germanotta found out when she tried to use her personal time and limited income to spread word about the SGBand. "I would make demo tapes and send them around," she eventually recounted. "Then I would jump on my bike and pretend to be [my] manager. I'd make $300 at work and [would] spend it all on Xeroxes to make posters [for the band]."[2]

Germanotta and her father went through a brief period when they didn't speak to or see one another due to their differences of opinion on the direction Germanotta's future was headed after she left school. "It wasn't really so easy for my dad," she later stated during a televised interview with journalist Barbara Walters, "especially in the beginning. We didn't talk for months after the first time he saw me play, and my mother told me he was afraid I was, like, mentally unstable."[3]

While her father's reaction stung, she refused to give up hope that her efforts since leaving college were in vain. Germanotta continued performing throughout New York City and promoted her band whenever and however she could. Her dedication was about to pay off in a Manhattan club called the Cutting Room shortly before her twentieth birthday.

||||||||||||||||||||||||||||||||||||||||||||||||||

CATCHING A BREAK

In March 2006, Germanotta and her band took the stage at the Cutting Room, where singer Wendy Starland was also performing. When Starland first watched the SGBand, she wasn't exactly won over.

Starland, impressed by Germanotta's performance at the Cutting Room, started the future Lady Gaga down the path to stardom.

She described the band itself as "awful," and she didn't find their lead singer's appearance to be anything extraordinary.[4] Still, she was struck by something about Germanotta that convinced her the girl might be star material.

When the performance ended, Starland approached her and swore, "I'm about to change your life."[5] Nor did Starland waste any time making good on that promise. As soon as the pair of singers left the Cutting Room, Starland phoned a producer she was working with, Rob Fusari.

Fusari was 38 years old and from Parsippany, New Jersey. He had successfully produced several rhythm and blues (R & B) hits with talent including Destiny's Child and Will Smith. Before Germanotta's March performance at the Cutting Room, he had told Starland he was on the hunt for a female singer for a band similar to the Strokes. Fusari emphasized that the performer he was seeking didn't have to be physically or vocally

PITCHING THE GIRL ||||||||||||||||||||||||||||||||||||||||||||||||||||||||||||

Fusari was a bit surprised when Starland woke him in the middle of the night to chat about an unknown singer she had just heard perform at the Cutting Room. Starland later recounted their first conversation about Germanotta. She recalled:

> "Rob said, "Why are you waking me up?" I said I found the girl. [He answered,] "What? It's really one in a million.

What's her name?" [I told him it was] Stefani Germanotta. [He responded with,] "Um, you gotta be kidding me. What does she look like?" [I told him not to] worry about that. [He asked,] "Does she have any good songs?" [I told him] no. [He asked,] "How is her band?" I told him, "awful." I wasn't pitching a product. I was pitching the girl."[6]

stunning. There just had to be something about her that made her shine and allowed her to captivate an audience. Starland was confident Germanotta matched the producer's description perfectly. Not long after she pitched Germanotta to Fusari, he agreed to meet with her.

Like Starland, Fusari wasn't instantly inspired by Germanotta's appearance. At that point in time, there was very little about her that screamed "rock star." Fusari's opinion changed, however, when Germanotta seated herself at his piano and unveiled the same powerful and captivating presence that had awed Starland. Though he was impressed, he immediately realized Germanotta wasn't quite right for the Strokes.

"Stefani's confidence filled the room. Her presence is enormous. And fearless. I listened for the pitch, the tone, and timbre of her voice. Was she able to have a huge dynamic range? Was she able to get soft and then belt? And I felt that she was able to do all that while giving out this very powerful energy."[7]

—STARLAND DISCUSSING WHAT ABOUT GERMANOTTA MADE HER DECIDE TO PHONE FUSARI

Initially, producers were wary of Germanotta's unique performance style, but they couldn't deny her talent.

"I thought she was a female [version of Beatle] John Lennon," Fusari noted. "She was the oddest talent."[8] Odd or not, she made a lasting impression on the producer. He decided to start collaborating with Germanotta—a move that inched her closer to the rock-and-roll stardom she had always dreamed of.

||||||||||

Fusari influenced Germanotta's decision to make dancing a large part of her performances.

CHAPTER 4

Big Changes

t didn't take long for Germanotta and Fusari to form a close professional and personal relationship. She saw him as a mentor, a fellow artist, and ultimately, a boyfriend. They collaborated on what direction her career should take and what performance style was most likely to accelerate her rise to stardom.

At first, the pair worked on rock music similar to songs put out by bands such as Nirvana and Led Zeppelin. They also toyed with the idea of billing

Germanotta as a singer-songwriter who composed piano ballads, in the fashion of pop artists such as Michelle Branch and Avril Lavigne. Yet both Fusari and Germanotta soon realized she didn't quite match the performance stereotype of someone who, as Starland described, was "classically beautiful, very steady, and more tranquil."[1] Since Fusari didn't envision his girlfriend topping the charts with either rock hits or piano ballads, he had to find another performance mode that was a better fit.

He stumbled upon inspiration in a *New York Times* article about folk-pop star Nelly Furtado. Fusari read that Furtado's producer had done wonders for her career by transforming her into a dance artist. Germanotta wasn't initially thrilled by Fusari's idea to do the same for her, but she agreed to give it a try. She also began working with a drum machine.

Meanwhile, Fusari coached her on a few other changes he believed would quicken her rise to fame. For starters, he objected to a lot of Germanotta's fashion choices. He believed being a star meant dressing like one—all the time. As Fusari explained, her typical working wardrobe, which consisted of a sweatshirt and leggings, didn't make her look the part.

"Prince doesn't pick up ice cream at the 7-Eleven looking like Chris Rock," he reminded her. "You're an artist now. You can't turn this on and off."[2] Once again, Germanotta heeded her producer's advice and started wearing shorter skirts. After a while, she dropped the skirts altogether and began dressing in only underwear or tights.

A large part of reinventing Germanotta's identity also involved changing her name. Both she and Fusari felt "Stefani Germanotta" didn't do much to sell the image of a glamorous rock star. Multiple

KEEPING IT PROFESSIONAL

Germanotta's relationship with Fusari could be complicated at times. Since they worked together in addition to dating one another, the line between their personal and professional roles often became blurred. For example, when Fusari gave Germanotta advice on how to dress, she would grow defensive and act as if her feelings had been hurt. Similarly, when he told her he thought they should start using a drum machine, she accused him of not having confidence in her abilities as a performer. Though they ultimately broke up, Fusari continued to be involved in Germanotta's career.

Just as her classmates in high school noted, Lady Gaga's acquaintances years later emphasized that she offered constant support and encouragement, even as she herself struggled to succeed. "She tried to make everyone feel good," noted DJ Brendan Sullivan. "I'd go to her apartment with my unpublished novel, and she would tell me that I was the most brilliant writer of my generation, the poet laureate of the Lower East Side. No one else was doing that for me."[3]

stories attempt to explain how the Italian-American Catholic schoolgirl came to be called Lady Gaga. Each story is a little bit different. One of the most popular versions features Fusari singing a song called "Radio Gaga" by the British rock band Queen whenever Germanotta walked into his studio. Another account involves a text message from the producer getting scrambled so that "Radio Gaga" read "Lady Gaga" in the subject line. Whatever the source of Germanotta's new stage name, "Lady Gaga" it was. Though she had yet to make it big, a star had been born.

DREAMS AND DASHED HOPES

Lady Gaga's new name and new look didn't guarantee her top billing. She and Fusari had composed a song called "Beautiful, Dirty, Rich." Now the trick was scoring a record deal. Fusari wasted no time arranging for managers from various record labels to watch Lady Gaga perform the number in 2006.

"Beautiful, Dirty, Rich" was inspired by Lady Gaga's former classmates at NYU who routinely asked their wealthy fathers for handouts. Much to Lady Gaga's delight, the record label group Island Def Jam took interest in the piece and her performance. The president of the company, L. A. Reid, assured her she was well on her way to becoming a star and offered her a more-than-tempting $850,000 record deal. However, the management of Island Def Jam failed to make good on their promises of success.

Fusari worked with Lady Gaga to produce tracks for the label, but Reid began canceling business dinners. He had reportedly changed his mind about the young performer he had previously been so enthusiastic to sign. It looked as if Lady Gaga wasn't going to enjoy her first recording contract with Island Def Jam after all.

The news tore her apart. Lady Gaga had never been naive about the challenges of creating a name for herself as a rock star, but she had always remained determined to overcome them. For the first time ever, her confidence was seriously shaken. Could she overcome the pain of her first failed record deal? Did she really have the talent and star power to back up the bold glamour of her new identity?

"I went back to my apartment on the Lower East Side, and I was so depressed," Lady Gaga later recalled of her reaction to Reid's change of heart.[4] Nevertheless, she also noted that the sting of his rejection spurred a new chapter of her life as a performer. "That's when I started the real devotion to my music and art."[5]

NEW DIRECTIONS

After losing the deal with Island Def Jam, Lady Gaga decided it was time for a few more life changes. She and Fusari eventually ended their romance, and she became involved with a drummer, Luc Carl. The 29-year-old musician also managed the rock bar Saint Jerome's, which happened to be a popular hangout for hard-rock performance artist Lady Starlight.

Soon Lady Starlight and Lady Gaga began collaborating, ultimately presenting "Lady Gaga and the Starlight Revue: The Ultimate Pop Burlesque Show" on the New York club scene. When they weren't performing in their stage production, which mainly included 1970s music, the pair opened for various glam rock bands, such as the Semi Precious Weapons. The duo's onstage costume choices could be outlandish, with bikinis

THE BIRTH OF A PERFORMANCE ARTIST

According to Lady Gaga, it was Lady Starlight who first inspired her to think as a performance artist. "One day [Lady Starlight] was like, '[Our show's] not really a concert, and it's not really a show," she recalled. "'It's performance art. What you're doing is not just singing: it's art.' And once she pointed out to me what I was already doing, I just started analyzing that more and researching to try to take it in a different direction. And that's really what we did."[6]

A NEW ROUTINE OR *ROCKY HORROR?*

When Fusari saw Lady Gaga performing with Lady Starlight, he was stunned by their routine—and not in a good way. "It was *Rocky Horror* meets eighties band, and I didn't get it at all," he later recounted.[7] *The Rocky Horror Picture Show* is a 1975 musical horror comedy/rock opera film about vampires from another planet. It features outlandish plot lines and a main character who dresses in drag. "I told Stefani that I could get her another DJ," Fusari said he mentioned to Lady Gaga after watching her performance. "But she was like, 'I'm good.'"[8]

and fingerless black gloves typically making up their wardrobe selections.

Go-go dancing and a strict diet led Lady Gaga to lose a great deal of weight during this time. She also claims she started experimenting with cocaine, though friends say they never saw her using drugs. Either way, Lady Gaga's parents and close acquaintances, including Fusari, expressed concern over the direction her career—and life—seemed to be taking.

In spring of 2007, Fusari tried to find Lady Gaga another opportunity to land a record deal. He managed to arrange a meeting in Los Angeles,

Lady Gaga and Lady Starlight
perform in 2007.

DOES LADY GAGA DO DRUGS?

Along with rejection, Lady Gaga also claims to have struggled with drugs early in her career. She by no means glamorizes the experience, nor does she encourage fans to model her behavior. Yet she also recently admitted she still uses sometimes. She explained:

"I won't lie; it's occasional. And when I say occasional, I mean maybe a couple of times a year. [But] I do not want my fans to ever emulate that or . . . think they have to be that way to be great. It's in the past. It was a low point, and it led to disaster."[10]

California, between her and Jimmy Iovine, the chairman of Interscope Records. At first, it seemed like history was on the verge of repeating itself when Iovine didn't show up for the conference. Disappointed, Lady Gaga and Fusari headed back to New York, where they were asked by Interscope to return to Los Angeles in a few weeks.

As fate would have it, this second visit proved more successful. Famous for having an ear for music, Iovine carefully listened to some of Lady Gaga's tracks. After he thought about what he had heard, Iovine decided not to follow in Reid's footsteps. The executive declared, "Let's try this," and Lady Gaga prepared to begin working at Interscope.[9]

||||||||||

Jimmy Iovine's decision to sign Lady Gaga to Interscope Records was one he would not regret.

In an effort to further distinguish herself from other artists, Lady Gaga dyed her hair blonde.

CHAPTER 5

Finally Finding Fame

||||||||||||||||||||||||||||||||

Lady Gaga moved to California in early 2008 to launch her career with Interscope Records in Santa Monica. Initially, the record label company had her write songs for better-known music artists including Britney Spears, New Kids on the Block, and the Pussycat Dolls. Meanwhile, she also recorded tracks with a producer called RedOne.

Even after successfully signing to Interscope, however, Lady Gaga continued to have doubts about whether she fit the image of a real-life rock star. She mainly wondered whether the company considered her attractive enough to appeal to audiences. At the same time, producers expressed concern that her dark hair and overall appearance was too strikingly similar to performer Amy Winehouse. The British singer-songwriter was known for her unusual mix of soul, jazz, and R & B hits, but she was also famous for her drinking, drug use, and unpredictable behavior. Eager to please her record label company and simultaneously develop her own unique identity as an artist, Lady Gaga agreed when one producer asked her to dye her hair blonde.

She also started to become obsessed with deceased pop artist Andy Warhol, who had focused

THE WORDS OF ANDY WARHOL ||||||||||||||||||||||||||||||||||||||||||

Lady Gaga's obsession with Warhol drove her to purchase countless books on the pop artist. Not only did she read about his life and work but she also began using what she learned as a guidepost for her own journey toward fame. "Andy's books became her bible," noted one of Lady Gaga's friends. "She would highlight them with a pen."[1]

Lady Gaga visited the Andy Warhol exhibit
at the Grand Palais museum in Paris, France, in 2009.

several of his prints, paintings, and films on the
themes of fame and famous people. After studying
Warhol's life and work, Lady Gaga began to arrive
at the conclusion that fame itself was a type of
art. This new way of thinking provided her with
fresh opportunities to explore her identity as a

performer—and especially as one who hoped to ultimately become famous. After being inspired by Warhol, she felt more comfortable inventing the performance artist audiences would eventually flock to see onstage.

|||||||||||||||||||||||||||||||||||||||||||||||||||||||||

A DEBUT SINGLE

As Lady Gaga developed new attitudes toward fame, stardom, and her identity, she worked on what turned out to be her first hit song in 2008. *New York* magazine journalist Vanessa Grigoriadis later described "Just Dance" as "global-dance-party music—faster beats, synth sounds, [and] an ethos that made sense to [Lady Gaga's] hippie heart."[2] The song also made sense to other performance artists. In particular, big-name R & B singer Akon was deeply impressed with what he heard. Along with RedOne, he started collaborating with Lady Gaga on the track.

Akon's enthusiasm prompted Interscope executive Jimmy Iovine to take bigger steps to back Lady Gaga as she prepared to debut her first album, *The Fame.* For starters, she was invited to record at the home studio of Martin Kierszenbaum,

R & B sensation Akon has the utmost respect for Lady Gaga. In addition to contributing vocals to "Just Dance," he played an important role in getting Interscope to help her develop *The Fame*. Less than a year after the album was released, Akon offered the following words of praise when discussing Lady Gaga: "At this point, she deserves every bit [of fame]. . . . She's brave. She's fresh. She's different. She's bold. . . . You gotta take her as she is. That's the beauty of it. You're forced to like her the way she is without no extra stuff added."[3]

who was another Interscope executive. In addition, she started working on her dancing with a professional choreographer.

At the time, however, the question remained whether all these measures would be enough to transform "Just Dance" into a hit. By that point, rap was still all the rage in the United States. Lady Gaga's single was electropop. This music style was popular in several European countries, but it soon became clear that US audiences might be slower to warm up to a new electropop performer.

Realizing radio stations were reluctant to air her single after it was released in April 2008, Lady

Mainstream audiences and radio stations didn't immediately accept Lady Gaga's electropop sound and outrageous costumes.

Gaga rose to the challenge and began touring music clubs. She did not disappoint her growing fan base. Glitter, wigs, disco-era clothes, and a

Lady Gaga, Akon, and RedOne were aware that electropop wasn't exactly in fashion in the United States as they worked on "Just Dance." In a way, that fact appealed to them. They were confident the single would be embraced in Europe and other parts of the world. Fueled by Lady Gaga's stylings, RedOne suspected "Just Dance" would ultimately win over US audiences—and bring fans of all backgrounds together. "Gaga and I believe that the world needs this music," he declared. "That it is a way to unite."[5]

DJ named Space Cowboy were all part of Lady Gaga's glamorous—if slightly over-the-top—stage presence. As her name and reputation as a performance artist grew, so did her confidence that she would indeed achieve the fame she had dreamed of as a girl. She explained the feeling:

> It's as if I've been shouting at everyone. And now I'm whispering, and everybody's leaning in to hear me. I've had to shout for so long because I was only given five minutes, but now I've got fifteen. Andy [Warhol] said you only needed fifteen minutes.[4]

||||||||||||||||||||||||||||||||||||||||||||||||||||||||||||||

A creative team known as Haus of Gaga helps Lady Gaga envision and create her outrageous hair, makeup, and wardrobe choices that dazzle audiences onstage. She hired her own handpicked assortment of stylists, makeup artists, and designers after she began achieving success with Interscope. The men and women who make up this team also work with Lady Gaga to develop many of the props and sets that are so pivotal to her performances.

EARNING ACCLAIM WITH ELECTROPOP

As it turned out, Lady Gaga got far more than 15 minutes, thanks to "Just Dance" and *The Fame*, which was released in August 2008. Throughout much of that year, her appearances at music clubs—and the splash that those appearances created—led to the album and single becoming her breakthrough achievements. At the same time, however, "Just Dance" didn't reveal itself as a chart topper in the United States overnight.

When Lady Gaga toured in other countries, fans ate up what RedOne described as "essentially a rock track but with synths instead of guitars."[6] "Just Dance" quickly topped the singles tallies in

Australia, Canada, Ireland, and the Netherlands. Yet US crowds took a bit more time to help it rocket to a leading position on charts. Eventually, though, they proved their loyalty to Lady Gaga and her new sound.

As Lady Gaga toured US radio stations, more DJs began playing "Just Dance." By January 2009, Lady Gaga's single clinched the Number 1 spot on both US and United Kingdom (UK) charts. *The Fame,* which features an additional 12 tracks besides "Just Dance," added to her acclaim. Critics gave the album mixed reviews, with some praising

DANCING THROUGH THE DARK TIMES

The lyrics of "Just Dance" talk about being intoxicated at a club. However, Lady Gaga explained the point of the song is not necessarily to encourage her fans to drink or use drugs. She wrote the song shortly after leaving New York for California—a move she says resulted in her being "taken very quickly out of [a] party lifestyle."[7]

Lady Gaga emphasized that the music and lyrics are supposed to encourage people to dance through the tough times in their lives. For some, that may mean losing a job or a loved one. For others, it could mean struggling with drug or alcohol issues. "If you've ever been so high that it's scary, the only way you can deal with it is not deal with it," she notes. "So you just kind of dance through the intoxication."[8]

her for a "well-crafted sampling of feisty anti-pop in high quality" and others panning her for uneven vocals and a lack of originality.[9] Yet regardless of whether she was complimented or criticized, Lady Gaga was undeniably growing more famous. This was rather appropriate, given that her debut album focused on the concept of fame itself. Lady Gaga explained:

> [The Fame] is about how anyone can feel famous. Pop culture is art. It doesn't make you cool to hate pop culture, so I embraced it, and you hear it all over The Fame. But it's a sharable fame. I want to invite you all to the party. I want people to feel a part of this lifestyle.[10]

||||||||||

Lady Gaga's first album is based on the idea of fame and pop culture, and in 2009, it was starting to garner worldwide attention.

Lady Gaga performs at the
2010 Grammy Awards.

CHAPTER 6

Celebrity and Monsters

||||||||||||||||||||||||||||||||||||||||||||||||||||||||

espite earning mixed reviews from music critics, Lady Gaga made it to the big time, thanks to *The Fame*. She ultimately received five Grammy nominations and, on January 31, 2010, opened the awards ceremony by performing with big-name British singer-songwriter Elton John. As attention grabbing as ever, Lady Gaga and her partner stole headlines for giving "a torchy duet, complete with ashes,

[fake] severed limbs, and some seriously flashy jewelry."[1] Later that evening, she took home the Grammy for Best Electronic/Dance Album. Lady Gaga scored another win for the single "Poker Face," which is one of the tracks featured on *The Fame*. The song earned an award for being the Best Dance Recording that year.

Other honors brought Lady Gaga further acclaim, including 13 MTV Video Music Award (VMA) nominations. In addition, she made history when four of the songs from her debut album became Number 1 hits. "Just Dance," "Poker Face," "LoveGame," and "Paparazzi" all held a reigning position atop US charts.

These achievements left little doubt that Lady Gaga was a hot new artist on the US music scene, not to mention on an international scale. Yet a great deal of mystery continued to surround the glamorous and unpredictable performer. It was not uncommon for her to be compared to other sensational pop celebrities, including Madonna and Michael Jackson. On the other hand, not everyone knew quite what to make of the splashy—and always interestingly costumed—Lady Gaga.

Lady Gaga is aware that her wardrobe and overall stage presence have generated a lot of speculation about who she is and what she's truly like. Yet she insists she's really not that much of a mystery. "Photographers say . . . 'I want to photograph the real you,'" she noted during an interview. She responded,

"I'm like, 'What . . . are you looking for? I'm right here. You've seen me with no makeup. You've asked me about my drug history, my parents, my bank account. . . . This is what I'm really like. This is exactly what I'm really like.'"[2]

UNAFRAID TO BE EXTREME

Fascination with the artist grew at a steady pace. Leather, sequins, glitter, and outlandish eye makeup regularly found their way into her wardrobe. Her onstage attire included everything from fake blood to bikinis. Some critics praised her bold and seemingly shameless fashion sense. Other critics cringed at it. Either way, Lady Gaga didn't seem to be overly concerned with any negative feedback about her physical appearance. For her, audiences' shocked reactions and the click of photographers' cameras appeared to be part of the response she was looking for. As she explained to the press:

> I'm not super-sexy. A girl's got to use what she's given, and I'm not going to make a guy drool the way a Britney [Spears] video does. So I take it to extremes. . . . What I do is so extreme. It's meant to make guys think: "I don't know if this is sexy or just weird."[3]

Regardless of what conclusion her fans drew, Lady Gaga's outlandish apparel and frequently bizarre props conveyed an important message: she was a performance artist. She went far beyond simply singing a tune onstage or dancing to electropop rhythms. Her music, words, and theatrical choices all blended to create a presentation that prompted audiences to think about things in new ways.

For example, *The Fame* focuses on the concept of experiencing fame and its long-lasting effects. To the shock of some fans, however, music videos and live performances sometimes showed Lady Gaga simulating her own death. As she explained, she chose to include this performance element because death and downfall are sometimes the price of celebrity and stardom. Whether audiences gasped at her being covered in fake blood or watched her being thrown from a balcony, her performances—combined with her music and lyrics—made an impact. *The Fame* would not be the last of Lady Gaga's work to achieve this effect.

|||||||||||||||||||||||||||||||||||||||||||||||||||||

USING HER FEAR AND ANXIETY

It was hard for some fans to imagine a successful, popular performance icon could be obsessed with and haunted by "monsters." Yet Lady Gaga was—or at least by very human fears, anxieties, and

THE DECAY OF A SUPERSTAR

Lady Gaga took the time to explain to journalist Anderson Cooper exactly why she chose to cover herself in fake blood while performing "Paparazzi" at the 2009 VMAs. According to the pop star, mimicking her own death onstage was a way of giving audiences what they want to see from anyone who's famous. From her point of view, people are inevitably fascinated by celebrities' failures, deaths, and downward spirals.

"That's what everyone wants to know, right?" Lady Gaga reflected. "What's she gonna look like when she dies? What's she gonna look like when she's overdosed. . . . Everybody wants to see the decay of the superstar."[4]

insecurities that she often referred to as "monsters." In fact, as her career progressed, the term *monster* began to appear more and more in her work. She affectionately referred to her fans as "little monsters."[5] A trademark performance move with her hand became known as the "monster claw."[6] She explained that it was emotional monsters that inspired her to get to work on her next album, *The Fame Monster.*

"I just felt this urgency to write about what I was going through—my fears and my monsters," she explained shortly after the album was released in November 2009. "I had been so ambitious and dreaming for so long that I wasn't feeling very much."[7] Lady Gaga explained during the same interview how being famous essentially forced her to deal with the intense emotions she had been blocking out. "To me, being an artist is being private in public," she said. "So I'm being private in public every night, and all my monsters and my fears went leaping out of me, and I just began to write."[8]

Lady Gaga felt at ease sharing some of her innermost anxieties with her fans. The monsters that revealed themselves through her efforts

The Fame Monster demonstrated Lady Gaga's ability to connect with her many fans by showing them her personal struggles.

revolved around everything from addiction to poor self-esteem to fear of death. Woven into eight tracks on Lady Gaga's newest electropop album, such concepts—combined with her performance artistry—appealed to audiences and critics alike. As one reviewer observed:

> She's not complacent with doing the same thing over again. She's willing to try new (and sometimes very unexpected) things, branching out at a time when it feels like every lone pop diva is more than willing to compromise [her] artistic growth just for the sake of having a radio hit.[9]

Besides being willing to take artistic risks, Lady Gaga was also determined to win over her fans. She made television appearances on everything from *Saturday Night Live* to *The Oprah Winfrey Show*, and

ROCKING OUT THE ROYAL WAY

Lady Gaga didn't exactly tone down her typical onstage spectacle when she performed before Queen Elizabeth II of the UK in December 2009. In fact, Lady Gaga dressed like sixteenth-century British royal Queen Elizabeth I. Lady Gaga wore a gown that sported a 20-foot (6-m) train made of bright red latex. The eye-catching extravaganza didn't end there. During the performance, Lady Gaga was raised 30 feet (9 m) in the air, where she proceeded to play the piano.

Costumes made of guns, a bikini that shot out fireworks, and a car that transformed into a keyboard were just a few of the highlights of Lady Gaga's Monster Ball Tour. A series of plastic and rubber dresses also contributed to her flashy and unforgettable performance. Finally, a giant puppet designed to look like a ferocious fish with tentacles and terrifying teeth routinely made an appearance onstage.

in November 2009, she took off on the Monster Ball Tour.

Intended to promote *The Fame Monster*, the nearly 18-month tour proved to be something of a roller-coaster ride for Lady Gaga. The running storyline of the performance was her and a group of her friends getting lost in New York as they tried to get to the Monster Ball. The dazzling stage effects, bizarre costumes, and electropop music provided audiences with an audiovisual experience rivaled only by her previous concert tour.

The show took its toll on Lady Gaga, however. She suffered from fatigue, jet lag, and the inevitable physical and emotional exhaustion to be expected from such an effort. In March 2010, she passed out onstage. Those close to Lady Gaga expressed concern, but she insisted it was a passing problem and emphasized that she was both "completely rejuvenated and excited."[10] In reality, she had every reason to be exhausted. But she also had every reason to be thrilled at the prospect of what she had accomplished in a few short years.

||||||||||

Lady Gaga is known for her bizarre costumes and props.

Lady Gaga accepts a Grammy Award for Best Pop Vocal Album on February 13, 2011.

CHAPTER 7

Famous Philanthropy Efforts

||||||||||||||||||||||||||||||||||||||||

Tracks from *The Fame Monster* secured Lady Gaga coveted positions across international charts—not to mention among other winners at music award ceremonies. Singles such as "Bad Romance," "Telephone," "and "Alejandro" were placed at or near the top of the charts in multiple countries, including the United

States. *The Fame Monster* eventually earned Lady Gaga six Grammy nominations, three of which resulted in wins on February 13, 2011. At the end of the ceremony, she claimed a Grammy for Best Pop Vocal Album. "Bad Romance" also landed her awards for Best Female Pop Vocal Performance and Best Short Form Music Video.

By the time she wrapped up her Monster Ball Tour in May 2011, Lady Gaga was 25 years old. Within a few short years, she had achieved fame beyond what most performers experience in their lifetimes. In the process of working on hit albums and going on international tours, she had also seen to it that the world understood she wasn't just glitz and glamour. Few people would deny

NOT SHORT ON NOMINATIONS

Lady Gaga made quite an impact at the 2011 Grammy Awards—and not just because she was carried down the red carpet in a giant egg. She claimed three Grammys, and she was nominated for three more. *The Fame Monster* was up for Album of the Year. The song "Telephone," which is among the album's tracks, features Lady Gaga teaming up with R & B/pop sensation Beyoncé and was nominated for Best Pop Collaboration with Vocals. Finally, "Dance in the Dark," which is also included on *The Fame Monster*, was in the running for Best Dance Recording.

that Lady Gaga knew how to put on a show. Once she entered the public spotlight, however, she also proved she grasped the importance of using her fame for a greater cause.

||||||||||||||||||||||||||||||||||||||||||||||||||||||||

GOODWILL TOWARD THE GAY AND LESBIAN COMMUNITY

In June 2010, Lady Gaga won an award that was perhaps not as well known as a Grammy but she nonetheless considered it a great honor to receive. The Gay and Lesbian Alliance against Defamation (GLAAD) presented her with the GLAAD Media Award for Outstanding Music Artist. Since the very beginning of her performance career, people had observed how Lady Gaga—who is openly bisexual—had become an icon to the gay and lesbian community. She had started out playing in several gay and lesbian clubs, and her gay and lesbian fans had cheered her on as she struggled to convince DJs to give "Just Dance" airtime. As a result, she swore never to forget their support. She explained:

The turning point for me was the gay community. I've got so many gay fans, and they're so loyal to me, and they really lifted me up. They'll always stand by me and I'll always stand by them. It's not an easy thing to create a fan base.[1]

Lady Gaga wouldn't disappoint anyone who heard her make this vow of solidarity with the gay and lesbian community. Once she achieved fame, she ferociously fought against the lack of

TACKLING DON'T ASK, DON'T TELL

Prior to fall of 2011, Americans who were gay, lesbian, bisexual, or transgender and part of the US military had to live in fear of dismissal from the military if they revealed their sexuality. They were not permitted to be open about their sexuality. This policy of Don't Ask, Don't Tell was a measure Lady Gaga repeatedly criticized at rallies for gay and lesbian rights. Though many celebrities raised a public outcry against Don't Ask, Don't Tell, she made a particularly passionate speech in September 2010, calling for the policy to be overturned. To a crowd in Maine, including US servicemen and servicewomen, she announced:

"There are amazing heroes here today. [Their] stories are more powerful than any story I could tell [or] any fight I've ever fought. . . . I'm here because Don't Ask, Don't Tell is wrong. It's unjust, and fundamentally, it is against all that we stand for as Americans."[2]

In September 2010, Lady Gaga called for the US military's Don't Ask, Don't Tell policy to be repealed.

social acceptance for gay, lesbian, bisexual, and transgender individuals. She also started attending and speaking at rallies, where she urged fans to contact politicians about overturning laws many believe discriminate against US citizens based on their sexuality.

Lady Gaga has been known to use the same shock value that is often a part of her performance art to draw attention to issues important to her.

In September 2010, for example, she wore an outfit made almost entirely out of raw meat to the VMAs. She said she hoped the meat dress would prompt people to think about human rights—especially those of members of the gay and lesbian community. Lady Gaga wanted to make a point that not fighting for these rights would leave otherwise proud and independent Americans as vulnerable and lacking in basic freedoms as meaningless lumps of flesh. "If we don't stand up for what we believe in," Lady Gaga declared, "and if we don't fight for our rights, pretty soon we're

FASHION OR CRUELTY?

Not everyone applauded Lady Gaga's meat-based apparel at the VMAs. In fact, the president of People for the Ethical Treatment of Animals (PETA) blasted her wardrobe choice, saying,

"No matter how beautifully it is presented, flesh from a tortured animal is flesh from a tortured animal. Meat represents bloody violence and suffering, so if that's the look they were going for, they achieved it."[3]

Lady Gaga responded that the dress was "certainly no disrespect to anyone [who] is vegan or vegetarian." She added that she considered herself to be "the most judgment-free human being on the earth" but acknowledged that the outfit "has many interpretations."[4]

Lady Gaga made a controversial fashion statement at the 2010 VMAs with a dress made of meat.

going to have as [many] rights as the meat on our own bones."[5]

OTHER IMPORTANT CAUSES

Lady Gaga's philanthropy efforts are not limited to the gay and lesbian community. She quickly gained a reputation for charity work to raise awareness

Cyndi Lauper appears with Lady Gaga
at an event supporting AIDS research.

about HIV/AIDS as well. In 2010, she and pop
singer Cyndi Lauper collaborated with MAC
Cosmetics to produce their own shades of Viva
Glam lipsticks. Money earned from the sale of the
makeup helped fund MAC's global campaign to
stop the spread of HIV/AIDS.

On multiple occasions, Lady Gaga also used her celebrity status to combat the suffering caused by natural disasters. For example, she took action shortly after a deadly earthquake ravaged the Caribbean island of Haiti in January 2010. That same month, Lady Gaga held a concert at the Radio City Music Hall in New York City to raise money for victims of the quake. Between ticket sales and profits she donated from her online store, she helped raise approximately $500,000 for the people of Haiti.

More than a year later, Lady Gaga stepped up to the plate on behalf of citizens affected by the fatal earthquake and tsunami that ravaged Japan

HELPING RAISE AWARENESS ABOUT HAITI

For Lady Gaga, helping the people of Haiti wasn't simply about donating money. As she explained to talk-show host Oprah Winfrey in January 2010, her philanthropy efforts were also intended to raise public awareness about what was happening on the Caribbean island. "Haiti's still suffering," she said. "I was in New York during [the terrorist attacks there] on 9/11, and . . . I just remember feeling [as if] nobody really understood. And I worry that young people don't know enough about what's going on [in Haiti]."[6]

Lady Gaga's charity efforts reach all over the world. In 2010, she performed at a concert in Tokyo to benefit people living with HIV.

on March 11, 2011. In this case, she designed and sold prayer bracelets via her online store. Once again, Lady Gaga promised that all proceeds from her efforts would benefit the men, women, and children whose lives had been forever changed by the disaster.

Lady Gaga's fame has undoubtedly allowed her to have a positive impact as a philanthropist that she might not have enjoyed without her celebrity stature. In fact, in 2011, *Forbes* magazine ranked Lady Gaga as one of the world's most powerful celebrities, not to mention one of its most powerful women. She has undeniably influenced performance art and fashion, but she has also used her star power to help others and stand up for her ideals. Lady Gaga knows how to grab people's attention, and that trademark skill has allowed her to capture public focus for more than just music. As she was famously quoted saying, "I'm just trying to change the world, one sequin at a time."[7]

||||||||||

A SIZABLE DONATION ||||||||||||||||||||||||||||||||||||||||||||||||||||||||||||||

Lady Gaga has also focused many of her philanthropy efforts on helping youth who are at risk of becoming homeless or who are already living on the streets. In the late spring of 2011, she teamed up with a charity called the Robin Hood Foundation (RHF) to aid SCO Family of Services. This organization assists New York families struggling with problems such as poverty and abuse. Together with the RHF, Lady Gaga donated $1 million to further the work performed by SCO.

Lady Gaga performs "Born This Way" on *Good Morning America* in May 2011.

CHAPTER 8

Born to Shine

||||||||||||||||||||||||||||||||||||||||||||||||||||||||||||||||||||||||||||||||||||||

With the winter of 2011—and three new Grammys—it seemed there was little chance of the world losing sight of its sequined pop princess any time soon. By that point, Lady Gaga had enjoyed a few years of hit songs, highly publicized performances, and considerable influence on everything from fashion to philanthropy. As a result, she probably could have played it safe by continuing to generate the same music

The Fame and The Fame Monster had proven her fans adored. Yet living a little on the edge had always been a part of Lady Gaga's identity, and her 2011 album, Born This Way, reflects that fact. She promised eager audiences the new album contains the best music she had ever created. Lady Gaga also explained some of the themes of the 14-track album, as well as what she hoped fans would take away from it. "This connection that we all share is something so much deeper than a wig or lipstick or an outfit," she noted. "Born This Way is about what keeps us up at night and what makes us afraid."[1] Lady Gaga went on to emphasize that she credited her fans with providing her with the inspiration to craft her third album. She said,

> It's really written by the fans. They really wrote it for me because every night they're funneling so much into me. So I wrote it for them. Born This Way is all about my little monsters and me, mother monster.[2]

Focusing on themes that range from religion to feminism, the album also deals with relevant social topics such as immigration and freedom. In presenting these concepts, Lady Gaga broke from the strict dance-club, electropop flavor that had

In 2011, Lady Gaga's little monsters camped out in Central Park before the rock star's *Good Morning America* performance.

characterized *The Fame* and *The Fame Monster*. She instead made great efforts to incorporate a wider array of musical influences. Opera, heavy metal, and mariachi are just a sampling of the styles that mingle with her electropop and dance rhythms to define *Born This Way*.

Lady Gaga described the work as "a marriage of electronic music with major . . . metal or rock and roll, pop, anthemic-style melodies with really sledge-hammering dance beats."[3] For his part, Akon observed *Born This Way* would allow her to take her music to the "next level."[4] As singles from the album started hitting shelves, audiences took a breath in, opened their ears, and waited to see if they agreed.

|||||||||||||||||||||||||||||||||||||||||||||||||||||||||

THOUGHTS ON THE THIRD ALBUM

The title single, "Born This Way," was released on February 11, 2011. Apart from making music history for selling more than 1 million copies in record time, it climbed to the top of the charts in 19 countries, including the United States. The singles "Judas" and "The Edge of Glory" were released a few months later to similar global acclaim.

The album itself debuted on May 23, 2011, and proved a chart topper in multiple countries. Lady Gaga fans were optimistic it would be slated for future Grammy nominations. For the most part, critics appear to share audiences' enthusiasm for *Born This Way.*

Rob Sheffield of *Rolling Stone* complimented Lady Gaga by writing, "The more excessive Gaga gets, the more honest she sounds."[5] Another reviewer noted, "Excess is Gaga's riskiest musical gamble, but it's also her greatest weapon. . . . She's making a convincing case that she's evolving into our most surreally brilliant pop star."[6]

A lesser number of critics expressed the opinion Lady Gaga was spreading her talent too thin. They felt the album headed in too many stylistic directions. Still others—especially those who were deeply religious or more conservative—bristled at her references to sexuality and Christian icons,

THE NEW GAY ANTHEM?

When the single "Born This Way" was released in February 2011, some listeners predicted it would become the new gay anthem. They based their opinions on bold, straightforward lyrics, including, "No matter gay, straight or bi/ Lesbian, transgendered life/I'm on the right track, baby/ I was born to survive."[7] Comedian and pop-culture expert Gabe

Liedman summed up the tone and overall point of the song by saying,

"She didn't waste any time with poetry. She kind of got right to the point. It's not subtle. There's no misinterpreting it. That's what she thinks: You're born this way, born this gay!"[8]

including Jesus Christ and Mary Magdalene. As had almost always been the case, however, Lady Gaga's goal was not to please mainstream masses with traditional music and lyrics presented in a traditional way. During the summer of 2011, the pop star hinted that she planned to organize a 2012 worldwide tour to promote *Born This Way*. Based on what she has offered up in the past, it seemed likely whatever performance she arranged would be eye catching, awe inspiring, and far from traditional.

GLANCING INTO GAGA'S FUTURE

Since the very beginning of her career, it's been nearly impossible to predict what Lady Gaga will do next. Guessing how much glitz or scandal

A SPIN ON CHRISTIANITY

Some of the tracks featured on *Born This Way* invited the fury of religious leaders around the world. Many took exception to her bold discussion of homosexuality in the title song "Born This Way." Others objected to her irreverent portrayal of biblical figures, including Mary Magdalene and Jesus Christ, in the music video for "Judas."

Lady Gaga emerges from an egg during a performance of "Born This Way" at the 2011 Grammy Awards.

she'll bring with her every time she walks onstage is difficult. The only truly certain thing about this twenty-first-century pop icon is she seems destined to continue making a splash on the world music scene—and to achieve fame and success in the process.

Lady Gaga doesn't just perform for teen and adult audiences. In fact, she recorded "Hello, Hello," a duet with singer-songwriter Elton John for the 2011 Disney flick *Gnomeo and* *Juliet.* Lady Gaga's voice can be heard in the song during the movie. However, Elton John sang the song solo in the release of the separately recorded sound track.

While scores of fans undeniably adore her, Lady Gaga's harshest critics are often appalled by her. It's true that her outlandish antics simply aren't for everyone, and especially not for those people who consider her vulgar or more rooted in sensationalism than real talent. On the other hand, her fearless self-expression and over-the-top performance artistry have won Lady Gaga an international spotlight. Combined with her musical and dramatic skills, these qualities have rendered her one of the world's most powerful celebrities. Yet she sees her countless fans and multiple achievements as far more than a source of income.

Lady Gaga has demonstrated she is able to use her sway to influence public opinion on everything from gay, lesbian, bisexual, and transgender rights to the meaning and price of fame. She has also made it abundantly clear she sincerely adores the crowds who hail her as a pop icon. In turn, she views her performance art not only as a way to express herself, but also as a means of changing the world and her fans' lives for the better. As Lady Gaga explained during a recent interview, the idea that her wild costumes and makeup mean she is simply after fame and attention is completely incorrect. "The truth is every bit of me is devoted to love and art," she insisted. She went on to say,

> I aspire to be a teacher to my young fans, who feel just like I felt when I was younger. I want to free them of their fears and make them feel [as if] they can create their own place in the world.[9]

TRYING OUT DIFFERENT TRADES

Lady Gaga has by no means limited her career to performance art. In early 2010, photography equipment manufacturer Polaroid appointed her creative director of a specialty line of its imaging products. In this role, she has codesigned a variety of innovative items, including special camera sunglasses, that are intended to target younger generations of customers. The glasses contain a special camera that can snap photos, which can then be displayed on the glasses' lenses. In addition, Lady Gaga announced in March 2011 that she had been hired to write a regular fashion column for *V* magazine.

Being a pop icon undoubtedly has its perks, but they're not all related to topping music charts or winning Grammys. For Lady Gaga, one of the highlights of being who she is revolves around the enduring legacy of using her performance artistry to impact how audiences think and feel. To explain her perspective, she once referenced her infamous bubble dress from her Fame Ball Tour.

"I can have hit records all day, but who . . . cares?" Lady Gaga added,

"[Yet] how wonderfully memorable 30 years from now, when [people will] say, "Do you remember Gaga and her bubbles?" Because, for a minute, everybody in that room will forget every sad, painful thing in their lives, and they'll just live in my bubble world."[10]

Thanks to her unique performance artistry and colorful personality, the chances are excellent that Lady Gaga will indeed achieve her goal.

One of Lady Gaga's goals as a performer is to help her audiences forget its cares.

TIMELINE

1986

Lady Gaga is born Stefani Joanne Angelina Germanotta in New York City on March 28.

1990

At four years old, Stefani learns to play the piano by ear.

2004

Germanotta graduates from Manhattan's Convent of the Sacred Heart School and enrolls in NYU's Tisch School of the Arts.

2007

Interscope Records chairman Jimmy Iovine hears Lady Gaga perform "Beautiful, Dirty, Rich" in the spring and decides to sign her.

2008

Lady Gaga moves from New York to California to begin working for Interscope.

2008

Lady Gaga's debut single, "Just Dance," is released in April.

2005

Germanotta leaves NYU to concentrate on becoming a rock star.

2006

In March, singer Wendy Starland introduces Germanotta to producer Rob Fusari.

2006

Germanotta begins using the name Lady Gaga.

2008

In August, Lady Gaga's debut album, *The Fame*, is released.

2009

"Just Dance" clinches the Number 1 spot on both US and UK charts in January.

2009

Lady Gaga begins her Fame Ball Tour in March.

TIMELINE

2009

Lady Gaga's second album, *The Fame Monster*, is released in November.

2009

In November, Lady Gaga begins her seven-month world tour, The Monster Ball.

2010

Lady Gaga collaborates to produce new shades of Viva Glam lipstick with the goal of using proceeds to stop the spread of HIV/AIDS.

2010

In September, Lady Gaga wears a dress made of meat to the MTV VMAs.

2011

Forbes ranks Lady Gaga as one of the world's most powerful celebrities.

2011

Lady's Gaga's first single from the album *Born This Way* (also titled "Born This Way") is released on February 11.

2010

2010

2010

In January, Lady Gaga holds a concert in New York City to raise money for victims of an earthquake that rocked Haiti.

On January 31, Lady Gaga wins two Grammy Awards.

In June, GLAAD presents Lady Gaga with the GLAAD Media Award for Outstanding Music Artist.

2011

2011

2011

On February 13, Lady Gaga wins three Grammys.

In March, Lady Gaga sells prayer bracelets to benefit victims of the Japanese earthquake and tsunami.

Lady Gaga's third album, *Born This Way*, debuts on May 23.

GET THE SCOOP

FULL NAME

Stefani Joanne Angelina Germanotta

DATE OF BIRTH

March 28, 1986

PLACE OF BIRTH

New York City, New York

ALBUMS

The Fame (2008), *The Fame Monster* (2009),
Born This Way (2011)

TOURS

The Fame Ball Tour (2009), The Monster Ball Tour
(November 2009–May 2011)

SELECTED AWARDS

- Won 2010 Grammy for Best Electronic/Dance Album for
  The Fame (2008)
- Won 2010 Grammy for Best Dance Recording for "Poker
  Face" (2008)
- Won 2010 GLAAD Media Award for Outstanding
  Music Artist

- Won 2011 Grammy for Best Pop Vocal Album for *The Fame Monster* (2009)
- Won 2011 Grammy for Best Female Pop Vocal Performance for "Bad Romance" (2009)
- Won 2011 Grammy for Best Short Form Music Video for "Bad Romance" (2009)

PHILANTHROPY

Lady Gaga has frequently championed the rights of the gay, lesbian, bisexual, and transgender community. She has also dedicated significant philanthropy efforts to raising awareness about HIV/AIDS, aiding victims of natural disasters, and helping families and young people impacted by poverty and homelessness.

"**The truth is every bit of me is devoted to love and art. I aspire to be a teacher to my young fans, who feel just like I felt when I was younger. I want to free them of their fears and make them feel [as if] they can create their own place in the world.**"

—*LADY GAGA*

GLOSSARY

burlesque—A theatrical style that often features comic spoofs and skits as well as striptease.

chart—A weekly listing of record sales.

choreographer—Someone who creates and arranges the specific movements and steps for a dance.

collaborate—To work together in order to create or produce a work, such as a song or an album.

debut—A first appearance.

disco—A type of dance music that was especially popular during the 1970s and that frequently features a regular bass beat.

DJ—A person who announces or plays popular recorded music.

drum machine—An electronic instrument used to imitate the sounds of a drum set.

electropop—A kind of electronic music made with synthesizers.

ethos—The distinguishing character, sentiment, moral nature, or guiding beliefs of a person, group, or institution.

Grammy Award—One of several awards the National Academy of Recording Arts and Sciences presents each year to honor musical achievement.

icon—A person viewed as a representative or symbol of something.

jet lag—The state of feeling ill or extremely tired after changing time zones during travel.

paparazzi—Aggressive photojournalists who take pictures of celebrities and sell them to media outlets.

performance artist—An artist who provides audiences with both a visual and dramatic performance.

philanthropy—An act of charity, such as a donation, for a humanitarian or environmental purpose.

pop—A commercial or popular style of music.

posh—Elegant or upper class.

producer—Someone who oversees or provides money for a play, television show, movie, or album.

pyrotechnics—Fireworks and other special effects using explosions.

record label—A brand or trademark related to the marketing of music videos and recordings.

rhythm and blues (R & B)—A kind of music that—especially in modern times—typically combines hip hop, soul, and funk.

signing—An artist agreement, by signing his or name, to a contract (such as a recording contract).

studio—A room with electronic recording equipment where music is recorded.

synth—An electronic musical instrument that produces a wide variety of sounds by creating and combining signals of different frequencies.

track—A portion of a recording containing a single song or a piece of music.

ADDITIONAL RESOURCES

SELECTED BIBLIOGRAPHY

Callahan, Maureen. *Poker Face: The Rise and Rise of Lady Gaga.* New York: Hyperion, 2010. Print.

Grigoriadis, Vanessa. "Growing Up Gaga." *New York Entertainment.* New York Media, 28 Mar. 2010. Web. 22 August 2011.

Herbert, Emily. *Lady Gaga: Behind the Fame.* New York: The Overlook, 2010. Print.

Jonathan Van Meter. "Lady Gaga: Our Lady of Pop." *Vogue.* Condé Nast, 10 Feb. 2011. Web. 22 August 2011.

Lester, Paul. *Looking for Fame—The Life of a Pop Princess: Lady Gaga.* London: Omnibus, 2010. Print.

FURTHER READINGS

Aloian, Molly. *Lady Gaga.* New York: Crabtree, 2012. Print.

Doeden, Matt. *Lady Gaga: Pop's Glam Queen.* Minneapolis, MN: Twenty-First Century, 2012. Print.

Edwards, Posy. *Lady Gaga: Me & You.* London: Orion, 2010. Print.

Tieck, Sarah. *Lady Gaga: Singing Sensation.* Edina, MN: Abdo, 2012. Print.

WEB SITES

To learn more about Lady Gaga, visit ABDO Publishing Company online at **www.abdopublishing.com**. Web sites about Lady Gaga are featured on our Book Links page. These links are routinely monitored and updated to provide the most current information available.

PLACES TO VISIT

The Grammy Museum

800 W. Olympic Boulevard, Los Angeles, CA 90015-1300
213-765-6800
http://www.grammymuseum.org
The Grammy Museum features several exhibits related to pop music, as well as the prestigious awards Lady Gaga has received on multiple occasions.

The Massachusetts Institute of Technology Museum

265 Massachusetts Avenue, Cambridge, MA 02139
617-253-5927
http://www.web.mit.edu/museum
This museum has an exclusive photograph of Lady Gaga that is part of its recently updated Polaroid exhibit.

The Rock and Roll Hall of Fame and Museum

1100 Rock and Roll Boulevard, Cleveland, OH 44114
216-781-7625
http://www.rockhall.com
This museum hosts an exhibit that features Lady Gaga's famous meat dress.

SOURCE NOTES

CHAPTER 1. DEBUT TOUR OR TRAVELING PARTY?

1. James Montgomery. "Lady Gaga Promises 'Life-Changing Experience' with Fame Ball Tour." *MTV*. MTV Networks, 4 Feb. 2009. Web. 27 June 2011.

2. Ibid.

3. Hattie Collins. "Lady Gaga: The Future of Pop?" *The Times*. Times Newspapers, 14 Dec. 2008. Web. 27 June 2011.

4. Ibid.

5. Ibid.

6. Ibid.

7. Whitney Pastorek. "Lady Gaga Live in L.A.: *EW* Photo Blog!" *EW.com*. Entertainment Weekly, 14 Mar. 2009. Web. 27 June 2011.

8. Jill Menze. "Lady Gaga." *Billboard.com*. Billboard, 4 May 2009. Web. 27 June 2011.

9. Jonathan Van Meter. "Lady Gaga: Our Lady of Pop." *Vogue*. Condé Nast, 10 Feb. 2011. Web. 22 August 2011.

10. "Lady Gaga's Pop Revolution Continues with 'LoveGame.'" *MTV*. MTV Networks, 13 Mar. 2009. Web. 27 June 2011.

11. Ibid.

CHAPTER 2. EARLY STEPS TOWARD STARDOM

1. Vanessa Grigoriadis. "Growing Up Gaga." *New York Entertainment*. New York Media, 28 Mar. 2010. Web. 22 August 2011.

2. "Lady Gaga—Monster Ball Tour." *LA.com*. LA.com, 2010. Web. 26 Aug. 2011.

3. "Lady Gaga: 'I Was Bullied at School.'" *Def Pen Radio*. Def Pen Radio,19 Aug. 2009. Web. 22 August 2011.

4. Vanessa Grigoriadis. "Growing Up Gaga." *New York Entertainment*. New York Media, 28 Mar. 2010. Web. 22 August 2011.

5. Ibid.

6. Ibid.

7. Ibid.

8. Ibid.

CHAPTER 3. CHASING HER DREAMS

1. Hollie McKay. "Lady Gaga: 'I Have Been Clubbing Since Childhood.'" *FOXNews.com*. FOX News Network, 4 Mar. 2009. Web. 22 Aug. 2011.

2. Vanessa Grigoriadis. "125 Minutes with Lady Gaga." *New York News & Features*. New York Media, 29 Mar. 2009. Web. 23 August 2011.

3. Jocelyn Vena. "Lady Gaga Says Her Dad Thought She Was 'Mentally Unstable.'" *MTV*. MTV Networks, 10 Dec. 2009. Web. 23 August 2011.

4. Vanessa Grigoriadis. "Growing Up Gaga." *New York Entertainment*. New York Media, 28 Mar. 2010. Web. 22 August 2011.

5. Ibid.

6. Ibid.

7. Ibid.

8. Ibid.

CHAPTER 4. BIG CHANGES

1. Vanessa Grigoriadis. "Growing Up Gaga." *New York Entertainment*. New York Media, 28 Mar. 2010. Web. 22 August 2011.

2. Ibid.

3. Ibid.

4. Ibid.

5. Ibid.

6. Emily Herbert. *Lady Gaga: Behind the Fame*. New York: The Overlook Press, 2010. Print. 45.

7. Vanessa Grigoriadis. "Growing Up Gaga." *New York Entertainment*. New York Media, 28 Mar. 2010. Web. 22 August 2011.

8. Ibid.

9. Vanessa Grigoriadis. "Growing Up Gaga." *New York Entertainment*. New York Media, 28 Mar. 2010. Web. 22 August 2011.

10. "Lady Gaga Admits She Still Does Drugs 'Occasionally.'" *US Weekly*. US Weekly, 2 Aug.2010. Web. 23 August 2011.

CHAPTER 5. FINALLY FINDING FAME

1. Vanessa Grigoriadis. "Growing Up Gaga." *New York Entertainment*. New York Media, 28 Mar. 2010. Web. 22 August 2011.

2. Ibid.

3. Jocelyn Vena. "Akon Calls Lady Gaga His 'Franchise Player.'" *MTV.* MTV Networks. 5 June 2009. Web. 24 Aug. 2011.

4. Vanessa Grigoriadis. "Growing Up Gaga." *New York Entertainment.* New York Media, 28 Mar. 2010. Web. 22 August 2011.

5. Ibid.

6. "'Just Dance' by Lady Gaga." *Songfacts.* Songfacts, n.d. Web. 24 Aug. 2011.

7. Ibid.

8. Ibid.

9. "*The Fame* [Bonus Track]." *Barnes&Noble.com.* Barnesandnoble. com, 2011. Web. 24 Aug. 2011.

10. "'Just Dance' by Lady Gaga." *Songfacts.* Songfacts, n.d. Web. 24 Aug. 2011.

CHAPTER 6. CELEBRITY AND MONSTERS

1. James Montgomery. "Lady Gaga Teams with Elton John to Open the Grammys." *MTV.* MTV Networks, 31 Jan. 2010. Web. 7 Sept. 2011.

2. "Lady Gaga on 'Mastering the Art of Fame.'" *60 Minutes.* CBS Interactive, 14 Feb. 2011. Web. 25 Aug. 2011.

3. "Lady Gaga: 'I'm Not Super-Sexy.'" *Metro.* Associated Newspapers, 21 Jan. 2009. 25 Aug. 2011.

4. "Lady Gaga on 'Mastering the Art of Fame.'" *60 Minutes.* CBS Interactive, 14 Feb. 2011. Web. 25 Aug. 2011.

5. James Montgomery. "Lady Gaga Calls *Born This Way* Her 'Most Innovative' Work." *MTV.* MTV Networks, 22 Dec. 2010. Web. 26 Aug. 2011.

6. "Artists' Sign Language." *MTV.* MTV Networks, 10 Jan. 2010. Web. 7 Sept. 2011.

7. Jocelyn Vena. "Lady Gaga Inspired to Write by Her Fears and Monsters." *MTV.* MTV Networks, 24 Nov.2009. Web. 25 Aug. 2011.

8. Ibid.

9. Evan Sawdey. "Lady Gaga: *The Fame Monster.*" *PopMatters.* PopMatters.com, 23 Nov. 2009. Web. 25 Aug. 2011.

10. Rennie Dyball. "Lady Gaga: 'Why I Passed Out Three Times.'" *People.* Time, 24 Mar. 2010. Web. 25 Aug. 2011.

CHAPTER 7. FAMOUS PHILANTHROPY EFFORTS

1. "Lady Gaga Bio." *World of Gaga.* World of Gaga, 15 Mar. 2011. Web. 26 Aug. 2011.

2. "Lady Gaga's 'Don't Ask, Don't Tell' Speech: The Full Transcript." *MTV.* MTV Networks, 20 Sept. 2010. Web. 26 Aug. 2011.

3. Jocelyn Vena. "Lady Gaga Meat Dress Draws Criticism from PETA." *MTV.* MTV Networks, 13 Sept. 2010. Web. 26 Aug. 2011.

4. Ibid.

5. "Lady Gaga Bio." *World of Gaga.* World of Gaga, 15 Mar. 2011. Web. 26 Aug. 2011.

6. Jocelyn Vena. "Lady Gaga Meat Dress Draws Criticism from PETA." *MTV.* MTV Networks, 13 Sept. 2010. Web. 26 Aug. 2011.

7. Beth Stebner. "Gaga's *Born This Way* Born Mediocre." *NBC LA.* NBCUniversal, 23 May 2011. Web. 26 Aug. 2011.

CHAPTER 8. BORN TO SHINE

1. James Dinh. "Lady Gaga Says *Born This Way* Will Be 'Greatest Album of This Decade.'" *MTV.* MTV Networks, 29 Nov. 2010. Web. 26 Aug. 2011.

2. James Montgomery. "Lady Gaga Calls *Born This Way* Her 'Most Innovative' Work." *MTV.* MTV Networks, 22 Dec. 2010. Web. 26 Aug. 2011.

3. Ibid.

4. Jocelyn Vena. "Lady Gaga to Release First *Born This Way* Single in February." *MTV.* MTV Networks, 1 Dec. 2010. Web. 26 Aug. 2011.

5. Rob Sheffield. "Lady Gaga's *Born This Way* Cranks Up the Crazy." *CNN Entertainment.* Cable News Network, 24 May 2011. Web. 26 Aug. 2011.

6. Caryn Ganz. "Lady Gaga: *Born This Way.*" *Spin.* Spin Media, 2011. Web. 26 Aug. 2011.

7. Jocelyn Vena. "Lady Gaga to Release First *Born This Way* Single in February." *MTV.* MTV Networks, 1 Dec. 2010. Web. 26 Aug. 2011.

8. Ibid.

9. Emily Herbert. *Lady Gaga: Behind the Fame.* New York: The Overlook Press, 2010. Print. 249–250.

10. Vanessa Grigoriadis. "Growing Up Gaga." *New York Entertainment.* New York Media, 28 Mar. 2010. Web. 22 August 2011.

INDEX

ABOUT THE AUTHOR

Katie Marsico is the author of multiple books for children and young adults. She specializes in reference works for the school and library market. Marsico worked as a managing editor in children's publishing for several years before becoming a full-time writer.

PHOTO CREDITS